The Moon

Dr Raman K Prinja

www.heinemann.co.uk/library

Visit our website to find out more information about **Heinemann Library** books.

To order:

☎ Phone 44 (0) 1865 888066

▤ Send a fax to 44 (0) 1865 314091

▭ Visit the Heinemann Bookshop at www.heinemann.co.uk/library to browse our catalogue and order online.

First published in Great Britain by Heinemann Library, Halley Court, Jordan Hill, Oxford OX2 8EJ, part of Harcourt Education. Heinemann is a registered trademark of Harcourt Education Ltd.

Editorial: Nick Hunter and Catherine Clarke
Design: Jo Hinton-Malivoire and AMR
Illustrations: Art Construction
Picture Research: Maria Joannou and
Debra Weatherley
Production: Viv Hichens

Originated by Dot Gradations Ltd
Printed in Hong Kong, China by
Wing King Tong

ISBN 0 431 15452 X
06 05 04 03 02
10 9 8 7 6 5 4 3 2 1

British Library Cataloguing in Publication Data
Prinja, Raman
The Moon. – (The universe)
1.Moon – Juvenile literature
I.Title
523.3

Acknowledgements
The Publishers would like to thank the following for permission to reproduce photographs: AKG London p. **5**; Calvin J Hamilton p. **20**; Getty Images (Stone) p. **27**; NASA pp. **4**, **7**, **23**, **24**, **28**, **29**; Science Photo Library pp. **6**, **9**, **10**, **13**, **14**, **15**, **16**, **18**, **19**, **21**, **22**, **25**, **26**.

Cover photograph reproduced with permission of Photodisc.

The author would like to thank Kamini, Vikas, Sachin and all his family for their support.

Every effort has been made to contact copyright holders of any material reproduced in this book. Any omissions will be rectified in subsequent printings if notice is given to the publishers.

Contents

Any words appearing in the text in bold, **like this**, are explained in the Glossary.

What is the Moon?

The Moon is a grey, rocky ball, about 3475 kilometres (2160 miles) across. It is about 385,000 kilometres (239,000 miles) from Earth. If you imagine a model where Earth is the size of a basketball, then the Moon would be a tennis ball. On this scale the two balls would be placed about 7 metres apart.

The Moon is the brightest object in the night sky. It is one of the most beautiful and easiest things to see from Earth. You will be able to see the Moon on most clear nights. Although the Moon seems to shine very brightly in the sky, it actually gives out no light of its own. The Moon **reflects** the light that comes from the Sun.

Earth's partner

Earth moves around the Sun once each year, and the path it takes is called an **orbit**. As Earth travels around the Sun, the Moon moves in an orbit around the Earth.

These two separate images of Earth and the Moon were taken by the Galileo spacecraft and put together to show the 'partners' side by side.

The Moon is Earth's partner in its journey around the Sun. It is sometimes called Earth's natural **satellite**, which is the name given to any body in the **solar system** that revolves around a planet.

A drawing of the great temple devoted to the Greek goddess of the Moon, Artemis.

What did ancient people think of the Moon?

The Moon was an object of mystery and beauty to ancient people. The ancient Greeks and Romans thought of the Moon as a beautiful and powerful **goddess**. The Greeks called her Artemis, and the Romans knew her as Diana. One of the largest Greek temples was built to praise their much-loved Moon goddess. In old Japanese stories, they believed an **emperor** lived on the Moon and looked down on Earth to keep it safe at night.

Patches on the Moon

Looking up at the Moon you can see light and dark patches on its surface. Hundreds of years ago people thought the dark patches were seas. So they became known as *maria*, which is a **Latin** name for seas. They are not really seas, and there have never been ships on the Moon. The *maria* are low flat areas. They were once filled with hot melted rock called **lava**, which flowed across the Moon billions of years ago.

The lighter patches on the Moon are rough and hilly. They are called **highlands**. The highlands have many **craters** that can be seen easily with a good pair of binoculars. The craters are bowl-shaped holes that were made when chunks of rock crashed on to the Moon from space. Many large craters are hundreds of kilometres wide.

The light and dark patches we can see on the Moon are the highlands and maria *on its surface.*

The Moon is closer to Earth than any other object in our **solar system**. Because of this, it is the only place other than Earth that people have been able to visit. You can find out more about these visitors and what they learned about the Moon later in this book.

Astronaut Buzz Aldrin, is one of only twelve people to have ever walked on the Moon.

Festive Moon

The Moon has been used in special celebrations, events and calendars. In some cultures every **full Moon** in a year had a different name and purpose. The full Moon in September was sometimes called Harvest Moon. It marked the time for the big harvest before winter. The full Moon in May was called Flower Moon as all the flowers were in bloom.

Does the Moon move?

The Moon travels around Earth in an **orbit**. It takes about 27 days to complete a lap around the planet, and moves at a speed of about 3700 kilometres per hour (about 2300 miles per hour). If an aeroplane flew at this speed, it would take only 1 hour 30 minutes to get from London to New York!

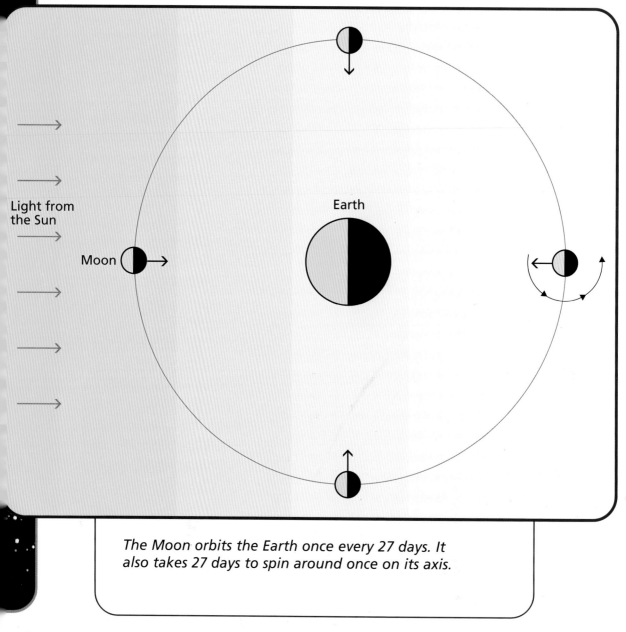

Light from the Sun

Moon

Earth

The Moon orbits the Earth once every 27 days. It also takes 27 days to spin around once on its axis.

The time taken for the Moon to go around Earth once is almost a month. The appearance of the Moon in the sky has been used to mark time in calendars for thousands of years. One example is the **lunar** month. This is the time taken to go from a phase of the Moon called a **new Moon** to the next new Moon. The lunar month is really about 29 and a half days long.

A spinning trick

If you look at the Moon for many nights in a row, you will always see the same light and dark patches on its surface. These are the patches of the *maria* and **highlands**, and you never see a different pattern of patches. It is as though the Moon never spins around to show its other side.

The Moon does spin, or **rotate**, on its **axis**, but it does this in a special way so that the same side of the Moon always faces Earth. This happens because the Moon spins on its axis in the same time that it takes to orbit around Earth. So in 27 days the Moon laps around Earth once, and it turns around on its own axis once.

This man is looking at a crescent moon, only 3 days into the lunar month.

The far side

The side of the Moon we cannot see from Earth is called the far side. Until spacecraft could reach the Moon, people did not know what the far side of the Moon looked like. Astronomers' telescopes could only see the side that faces Earth.

A Russian spacecraft called *Luna 3* (*luna* is the **Latin** word for moon) took the first pictures of the far side of the Moon in October 1959. It is much rougher and has many more **craters** than the side we always see from Earth.

This is a photo of the far side of the Moon, taken from the Apollo 16 *spacecraft in 1972.*

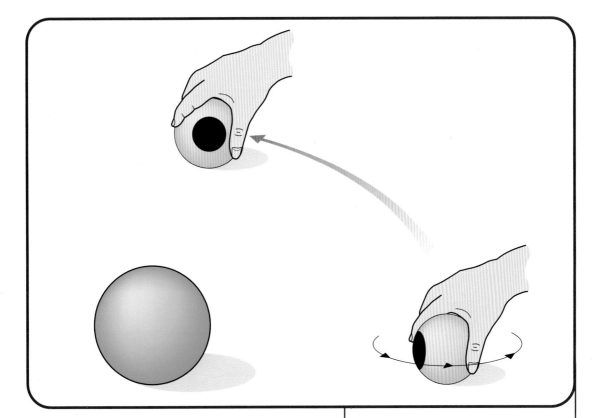

The Moon spins once during each orbit of Earth.

Try it for yourself

You can copy the Moon's spin using two balls. Put one on a table and let it be Earth. Draw a big spot on the other ball, which will be the Moon. Now move the ball with the spot as if it were **orbiting** Earth, but as you go make sure the spot always faces Earth (the other ball).

You'll see that to keep the spot facing Earth, you have to slowly spin the 'Moon' ball as it goes around the 'Earth' ball. You have to rotate the ball with the spot once every orbit.

Why does the Moon seem to change shape?

During a month you can see that the shape of the Moon in the sky changes. Sometimes it is a bright, full circle, other times it is half a circle, or even a thin, curved shape called a crescent. Sometimes you cannot see the Moon at all.

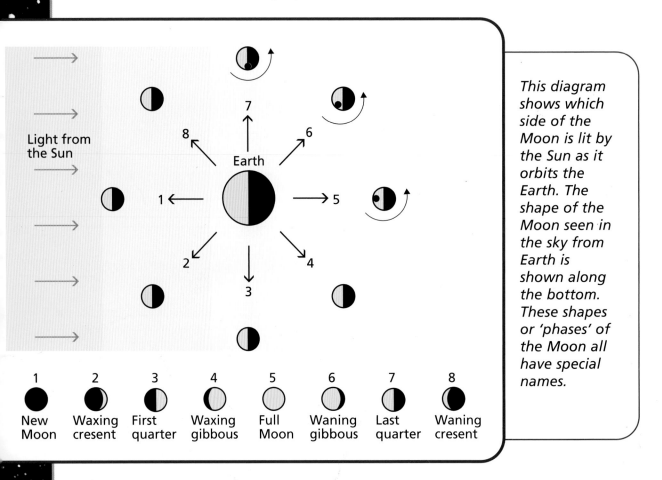

This diagram shows which side of the Moon is lit by the Sun as it orbits the Earth. The shape of the Moon seen in the sky from Earth is shown along the bottom. These shapes or 'phases' of the Moon all have special names.

1	2	3	4	5	6	7	8
New Moon	Waxing cresent	First quarter	Waxing gibbous	Full Moon	Waning gibbous	Last quarter	Waning cresent

Lighting up the Moon

The Moon isn't really changing its shape. It is just that we are seeing different parts of it being lit up. The Moon does not make its own light. Like all the other planets and moons in our **solar system**, the Moon acts like a giant mirror and **reflects** the light from the Sun.

Just like day and night on Earth, half of the Moon is always lit by the Sun while the other half is in darkness. As the Moon moves around Earth, we see different parts of the half that is lit by the Sun.

The different shapes in which the Moon appears to us are called phases. The phases of the Moon have special names which tell us how much of the lit up Moon we can see from Earth. The full **cycle** of phases of the Moon takes 29 and a half days to complete.

New Moon – when the Moon is lined up between the Earth and the Sun, the side of the Moon that faces us is not lit up by the Sun. This means that we cannot see the Moon at all, because it is too dark. This phase is called the new Moon.

Crescent – as the Moon moves in its **orbit** around Earth, a few days after the new Moon we can see a thin curved shape called a crescent. Slowly over the next few days this crescent shape grows thicker. The crescent getting larger is called a **waxing** Moon.

This picture shows a waning crescent Moon.

Half Moon (first quarter) – about one week after the new Moon, it has now completed a quarter of its **orbit** around Earth. At this time we can see half of the Moon's disc (or face) lit up by the Sun.

Gibbous Moon – the Moon continues to **wax** and soon more than half of it is lit up. This shape is called 'gibbous', which is an old English word that means humped.

The phase being shown in this picture is of a half Moon. The line dividing the sunlit side from the side in darkness is called the terminator.

Full Moon – about two weeks after the **cycle** started with a new Moon, the full sunlit face of the Moon can be seen. The Moon is a bright, full circle in the sky. Earth is now lined up between the Sun and the Moon. At most full Moons, the Moon passes either just above or just below the shadow of Earth cast by light from the Sun.

Third quarter – the Moon now enters the second half of its orbit around Earth. It starts to grow thinner each night. This is called a waning Moon. Its shape shrinks from full Moon down to a gibbous Moon again.

Half Moon – when it reaches the three-quarter point in its cycle, the Moon again shows us one half of the lit up face. We see half a Moon, but the half that is lit up this time is the one that was dark in the first quarter Moon.

Back to a new Moon – as it completes its journey around Earth, the Moon slowly becomes a waning (or thinning) crescent. Nearly a month after the start of the cycle, the phase is back to the invisible new Moon.

This time-lapse image shows the different phases of the lunar calendar and how the Moon appears to us at each stage. Compare this with the diagram on page 12, can you find the names of each phase?

Try it for yourself

You can see how the Moon has phases by using a lamp as the Sun and a light-coloured ball as the Moon. Remove the lampshade and place the lamp at one end of the room. Turn off all the other lights. Stand at the other end of the room, and hold the ball in front of you just above or below the plane of the lamp's light. Start with the ball between your face and the lamp. Now move the ball at arms length around your body (the Earth). As the ball orbits your body, turn your head to see how different parts of the ball are lit by the lamp.

What is an eclipse of the Moon?

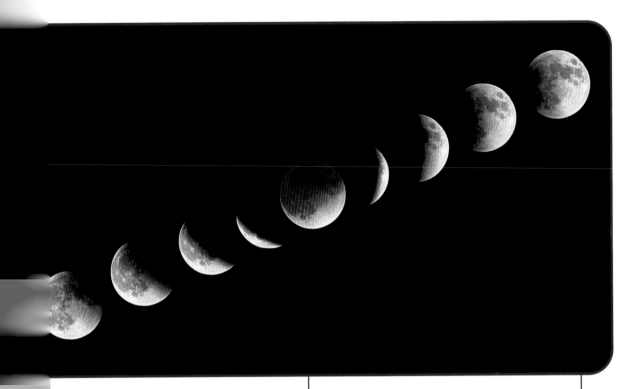

The stages of a lunar eclipse. The Moon slowly gets darker and turns a reddish colour when it is totally eclipsed.

A **lunar eclipse** (or total eclipse of the Moon) happens when Earth gets in the way and comes directly between the Sun and Moon. The three objects have to be lined up perfectly for an eclipse to happen. Lunar eclipses only happen when the phase is a **full Moon** and if the Moon passes through Earth's shadow.

A total lunar eclipse can be beautiful to watch. It happens about once or twice a year. Lunar eclipses are very safe to view without protecting your eyes. When an eclipse of the Moon occurs it can be seen by everyone on the side of Earth facing the Moon.

A full Moon that's dark!

During a total eclipse of the Moon, Earth blocks the Sun's light from striking the Moon. As the Moon slowly passes through Earth's shadow, the full Moon gets darker and darker.

After a couple of hours the Moon enters the darkest part of Earth's shadow, which is called the **umbra**. The Moon then goes almost completely dark. If astronauts were standing on the Moon at the same time that we were watching a total eclipse of the Moon from Earth, they would see Earth eclipsing, or blocking the light of, the Sun.

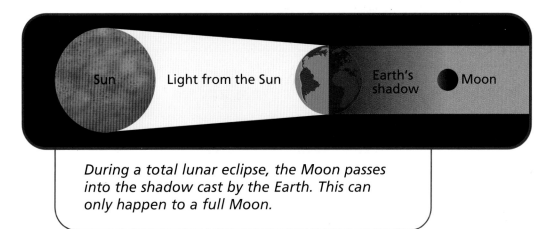

During a total lunar eclipse, the Moon passes into the shadow cast by the Earth. This can only happen to a full Moon.

A red Moon

The Moon is not completely black during a total eclipse. It can instead have some beautiful colours, and usually turns reddish brown. This happens because light from the Sun bends slightly as it passes through Earth's **atmosphere**. Some sunlight then passes around Earth and hits the Moon. The light is reddish in colour, just the way the sky is red near a setting Sun on Earth. This is because dust in Earth's atmosphere spreads the other colours that make up sunlight into different directions. The dust only lets the red part of the light pass through. How red the Moon is during a total lunar eclipse tells scientists how much dust there is in Earth's atmosphere.

What is the surface of the Moon like?

We know a lot about the Moon's surface because astronauts have landed there, and many rockets have been sent to study and photograph it. The surface of the Moon is almost covered in **craters**. There are around 500,000 craters on the Moon that are at least 1 kilometre (about half a mile) wide. The largest craters are surrounded by huge mountains, such as the Leibnitz mountains near the Moon's South **Pole**, which are about 2000 metres (1.2 miles) high.

Long, winding valleys are also found on the Moon. They were made by rivers of **molten** rock from **volcanoes** that flowed there billions of years ago.

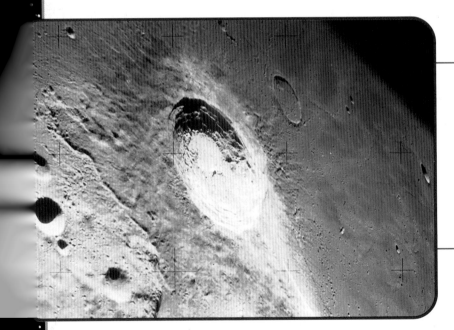

This huge crater on the Moon is called Aristarchus. It is 35 kilometres (21 miles) across.

No air, no weather, no life

The Moon is covered in a dry and powdery grey soil. Nothing lives there. There is no liquid water on the surface, and the Moon does not have an **atmosphere**. This means there are no clouds, rain or wind on the Moon.

Someone standing on the Moon would always see dark skies and never blue ones. Even during the day you would see a bright white Sun and the rest of the sky would be starry and black. This happens because the Moon does not have an atmosphere. On Earth, dust and gas in the atmosphere spreads different colours of sunlight to give us blue skies.

Mount Hadley on the Moon is 4.5 kilometres (almost 3 miles high).

Not much gravity either!

The force or pull of **gravity** on the Moon is six times weaker than on Earth. This is because the **mass** of the Moon is about 80 times smaller than Earth's mass. The more mass something has the greater the force of gravity. A boy or girl who weighs 30 kilograms on Earth would only weigh 5 kilograms on the Moon!

The Moon has such a weak gravity that it was never able to hold on to the layers of gas it would need to make an atmosphere. An atmosphere is like a protective blanket around a planet or a moon. This is why the Moon gets much hotter and much colder than any place on Earth. Midday temperatures at the Moon's **equator** can be as high as 130 °Celsius. All this heat escapes at night and it can get as cold as −170 °Celsius.

What is the Moon made of?

It has three main layers

The Moon is mostly made of rock. Like Earth, the Moon has three main layers. It has a stiff and strong upper layer called a **crust** that is at least 60 kilometres (37 miles) thick. Below the crust is a layer called the **mantle**. The mantle is the main rocky part of the Moon. Most of the mantle is a hard shell that is too cool to flow. At the centre of the Moon is a small solid **core** made mostly of iron. The core is about 680 kilometres (420 miles) across. It is mostly solid today, but may have been **molten** and liquid billions of years ago when the Moon was hotter.

There are moonquakes on the Moon, which are much weaker than the earthquakes on our planet. Scientists measure the moonquakes to discover more about the inner regions of the Moon.

mantle

core

crust

Like the Earth, the Moon has three main layers called the crust, mantle and core.

Is there any water on the Moon?

There are no seas or oceans of water on the surface of the Moon, but there may be ponds of ice (frozen water). Between 1996 and 1998 scientists sent two spacecraft to study the Moon very closely. They were called *Clementine* and **Lunar Prospector**.

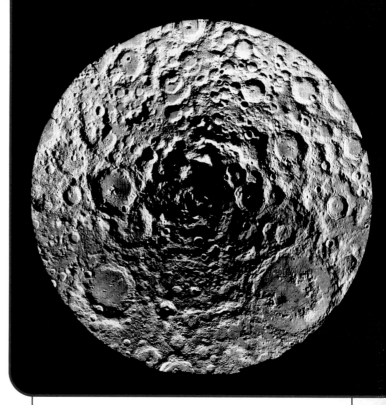

They found that water ice may be buried about 40 centimetres beneath the dry soil of the Moon.

A view of the South Pole of the Moon where water ice may be buried under the soil.

Scientists think that the ice is in deep **craters** at the North and South **Poles** of the Moon. It is in patches the size of ponds or lakes. Sunlight never reaches the floors of these craters. This is why the ice has never melted.

Where did the ice come from?

The ice on the Moon may have come from **comets** and **meteorites** that were mostly made of ice and crashed there billions of years ago. Finding ice on the Moon is very important. One day humans might be able to use it to make water on the Moon.

Where did the Moon come from?

Scientists are not sure how the Moon was made. The Moon is odd because it is only about four times smaller than Earth. Most of the other planets in the **solar system** are much larger than their moons. The largest planets, Jupiter and Saturn, are almost 25 times bigger than their largest moons. This means that Earth and its moon are a special pair in space.

The birth of the Moon

Our solar system was made about 5 billion years ago. It was made from a huge cloud of gas and dust. Some scientists think that soon after Earth was made, a vast chunk of rock smashed into it. This rock would have been about half the size of Earth. The powerful collision would have sent a huge amount of material flying into space.

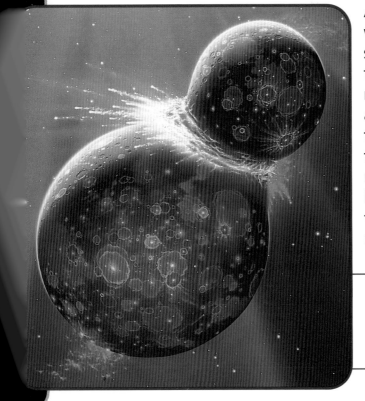

All the dust and rocks that were thrown out into space started **orbiting** Earth in a thick ring. Slowly the material in this ring cooled and started to clump together. Eventually all these clumps, and what remained of the rock that hit Earth, were pulled together by **gravity** to make our Moon.

This is an artist's idea of what the birth of the Moon might have looked like.

This picture, taken by the Galileo spacecraft, shows basins filled with lava that flowed billions of years ago on the Moon.

Why does the Moon look the way it does?

The newly formed Moon was itself struck by lots of huge rocks. They made many of the large **craters** and basins. During the first billion years, the Moon had **erupting volcanoes**. The dark coloured **lava** from these explosions filled some of the craters and basins. These are the dark patches we see today from Earth.

For the last 3 billion years the Moon has been cold and quiet. There are no more volcanoes exploding there today.

Has anyone visited the Moon?

One of the greatest adventures that many people dream about is going to the Moon. This dream came true for twelve lucky people who actually walked on the Moon. They were the brave astronauts of the Apollo missions.

The lift-off of the Apollo 11 *spacecraft. It landed the first men on the Moon in July 1969.*

The amazing Apollo missions

Between 1969 and 1972, the USA sent six spacecraft to the Moon. These spacecraft were called the Apollo missions. It took each rocket 3 days to fly the 385,000 kilometres (239,000 miles) to the Moon.

The Apollo spacecraft had two main parts. There was a command module and a **lunar** module. The command module stayed in **orbit** around the Moon, while the lunar module landed on the surface.

Working in pairs

The astronauts lived and worked in pairs on the Moon. They carried out experiments and took photographs of the surface.

The astronauts brought back rocks and soil from the Moon. Scientists on Earth have studied these samples. The rocks have taught us lots more about what the Moon is made of and how it has changed. No signs of life have ever been found on the Moon.

The first to get there

The first man to ever stand on the Moon was Neil Armstrong. He landed there on a spacecraft called *Apollo 11*, on 20 July 1969. When he first stepped on to the Moon he spoke the famous words 'That's one small step for man, one giant leap for mankind'. Neil Armstrong and all the other astronauts and scientists had shown the world the amazing things that humans can do.

In December 1972, the astronauts Eugene Cernan and Harrison Schmitt were the last people to visit the Moon's surface. No one has ever been back; at least not yet.

Who was Apollo?

These exciting missions to the Moon were named after a Greek god. In the **myths** of the ancient Greeks, Apollo was the son of the god Zeus. Apollo was a messenger for the gods and a fast runner. The USA's space agency **NASA** picked the name Apollo because this god rode through the skies in a magnificent golden chariot. They hoped their space missions to the Moon would be just as glorious.

This is the lunar rover used by Apollo 17 astronauts to slowly drive around the Moon.

Could I ever live on the Moon?

A painting showing how people might one day live and work on the Moon. They would look into the sky and see the Earth, in the same way that we see the Moon.

It is possible that people might one day be able to spend many years living and working on the Moon. Making a settlement or base there won't be easy or cheap though. The Moon is a harsh, lifeless place. It has no air, rain or oceans. We would have to learn how to get the oxygen and water we need. We'd also have to build houses and grow food and learn to protect ourselves from the Sun's harmful rays. Scientists from **NASA** have made some plans on how humans might survive on the Moon.

Robots first

The first spacecraft would send robots, not humans, to the Moon. The robots would explore the best areas to live on. Remote-control machines would be used to build oxygen-making factories to provide air for us to breathe.

Special materials would be sent there for making houses that are safe from the Sun's rays. The houses might even be buried under the ground to protect humans from the very hot and cold Moon climate.

Astronauts next

Small crews of astronauts would fly to the Moon next. They would make sure everything was working properly. They would check the houses, and the supplies of food, oxygen and water.

The first colony

Finally, the first human **colony** might settle on the Moon. Perhaps only a few hundred people might fly there first on a space aeroplane. They could live there for many years and learn about how to survive on the Moon. Fuel made on the Moon could be used to fly the space aeroplanes back to Earth.

Humans living on the Moon might seem like a dream today, but with a lot of hard work and money, this dream could come true in just 50 years time. One day you might even take a holiday to the Moon, or buy vegetables that were grown there!

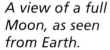
A view of a full Moon, as seen from Earth.

Fact file

Here are some important facts about the Moon:

Size – The Moon is nearly 3475 kilometres (2160 miles) across. It is nearly four times smaller than Earth.

Distance – The Moon is about 385,000 kilometres (239,000 miles) away from Earth. If you imagine a car travelling from Earth at a speed of 80 kilometres per hour (50 miles per hour), it would take 200 days to get there!

Gravity – The pull of **gravity** on the Moon is about one sixth of the pull on Earth, so you can jump six times higher on the Moon.

Spin – The Moon spins once on its **axis** in about 27 days.

Orbit – The Moon takes 27 days to **orbit** once around Earth.

Age – The Moon was made about 4500 million years ago.

Neil Armstrong is seen here, standing beside the Apollo 11 *landing module.*

This footprint, left by an Apollo astronaut on the Moon soil, will still be there in a thousand years time!

Temperature – The daytime temperature on the Moon can rise to more than 125 °Celsius, but at night it drops to –170 °Celsius.

Atmosphere – There is no **atmosphere**. Also no wind, weather or sound!

Craters – The largest **crater** on the Moon is on its South **Pole** and is called the Aitken Basin. It is more than 2100 kilometres (1300 miles) wide, and is 12 kilometres (7.5 miles) deeper than its surroundings.

Numbers
One thousand is written as 1000. One million is 1,000,000 and one billion is 1,000,000,000.

Glossary

atmosphere layers of gases that surround a planet

axis imaginary line about which a planet or moon spins

colony population or settlement of living things or people

comet small icy object made of gas and dust, which orbits around the Sun

core central part of an object, such as a planet or star

crater bowl-shaped hole made on the surface of a planet or moon by a rocky object crashing from space

crust outer, surface layer of a planet or moon

cycle set of events that repeat over a regular time

eclipse when one object passes in front of another, often blocking out light

emperor male ruler of a group of countries

equator imaginary line around the middle of a planet or moon

erupting volcano (see volcano)

full Moon when the Moon is seen as a complete circle in the sky

goddess female being that is worshipped

gravity force that pulls all objects towards the surface of the Earth, or any other planet, moon or star

highlands regions on the Moon that are above the level of the ground filled by lava

Latin language of the ancient Romans

lava molten rock that usually comes out of volcanoes

lunar to do with the Moon

mantle middle layer of a planet or moon, between the surface and the core

maria flat, plain regions of the Moon

mass amount of matter in an object, measured in kilograms

meteorites bits of material that enter Earth from space and fall to the ground

molten hot metal or rock that has melted to become a liquid

myths old stories told to explain how something came to be

NASA National Aeronautics and Space Administration. The organization in charge of the USA's space exploration activities.

new Moon phase when the Moon cannot be seen from Earth

orbit path taken by an object as it moves around another body (planet or star). The Moon follows an orbit around the Earth.

Poles points due North and South that mark the ends of the axis around which a planet spins

reflects when rays of light bounce off of an object

rotate turn or spin

satellite object that moves around a larger body (planet or star). Satellites can be natural, such as the Moon, or man-made.

solar system group of nine planets and other objects orbiting the Sun

umbra dark, inner part of a shadow

volcano opening in a planet's surface through which hot liquid rock is thrown up, during an eruption

waxing growing in size. The shape of the Moon increases during its cycle and this is known as a waxing Moon.

Further reading

Explore the Solar System: Moon, Giles Sparrow (Heinemann Library, 2001)

How the universe works, Heather Couper and Nigel Henbest (Dorling Kindersley, 1999)

Index